Comptroller of the Currency
Administrator of National Banks

Commercial Loans

Comptroller's Handbook
(Section 206)

Narrative - March 1990, Procedures - March 1998

Assets

Commercial Loans
(Section 206)

Table of Contents

Commercial Loans
Section (206)
Introduction

"Commercial loans" is a term commonly used to designate loans not ordinarily maintained by either the real estate or consumer loan departments. In asset distribution, commercial or business loans frequently comprise one of the most important assets of a national bank. They may be secured or unsecured and for short or long-term maturities. Such loans include working capital advances, term business loans, agricultural credits, and loans to individuals for business purposes.

Working capital or seasonal loans provide temporary capital in excess of normal needs. They are used to finance seasonal needs and are repaid at the end of the cycle by converting inventory and accounts receivable into cash. Such loans are normally unsecured, although recently more working capital loans are being advanced with accounts receivable and/or inventory as collateral. Firms engaged in manufacturing, distribution, retailing, and service-oriented businesses use short-term working capital loans.

Term business loans have assumed increasing importance in recent years. Such loans normally are granted for the purpose of acquiring capital assets, such as plant and equipment. Term loans involve greater risk than do short-term advances because of the length of time the credit is outstanding. Because of the greater risk factor, term loans usually are secured and may require amortization. Loan agreements on such credits normally contain restrictive covenants during the life of the loan.

In many banks, agricultural loans make up a large percentage of the commercial loan portfolio. The nature of the products involved in agricultural credits leads to a slow capital turnover rate. Whereas many businesses and industries experience gross sales in excess of invested capital several times a year, in farming it may take two or three years for gross sales to equal invested capital. For example, it takes several years for an orchard to bear enough fruit to enable the farmer to make a return on the investment capital. In spite of all the techniques and equipment at the farmer's command, acts of nature are beyond the control of even the best manager.

International Lending

A bank's international division lends to U.S. importers and exporters' foreign companies, multinational corporations, foreign banks, and foreign governments—either directly or through state entities. The terms of such lending are consistent with the purpose of the financing.

Short-term working capital loans commonly finance inventories or receivables arising from trade. Receivable pledges, warehouse receipts, and items on inventory or commodities may be held as collateral. However, in certain countries those forms of collateral are not legally recognized, and, therefore, the banks must be thoroughly familiar with the applicable local laws, regulators, and practices. Loans to foreign banks are usually short-term and unsecured.

Medium-term (1 to 5 years) lending generally represents capital goods financing, shipping loans and various specialized credits. Long-term loans (those exceeding 5 years) are normally used to finance extensive projects of multinational corporations, foreign governments, or foreign state-entities. Government guarantees of private long-term loans are common when the project has significant importance to a national economy.

The methods of loan financing in an international division are the same as those for domestic. Loans in international may be direct or discounted. In those instances, the bank holds a promissory note or similar instrument evidencing indebtedness. Current account advances, however, are a category of loans unique to international banking. That method of financing is an American substitute for the European method of financing by overdrafts. Current account advances are extensions of credit where no instrument of specific indebtedness is used. However, a signed agreement is on file stating the conditions applicable to payment made to the obligor. Other types of international financing treated as loans include own acceptances purchased (discounted), other bank acceptances purchased and discounted trade acceptances.

The same credit risks apply to international division loans as to those made in commercial loan departments. To this must be added country risk—the primary additional component that distinguishes an international loan from a domestic loan. Basically, country risk involves the possibility of a loan loss or a "locked-in" situation for the bank because of adverse political, economic and social developments, expropriation, the freezing of assets, balance of payments problems, imposition of exchange controls, foreign exchange rate fluctuations, devaluations, and inconvertibility. Country exposure is a cross-border risk whenever a bank lends to a borrower outside its national boundaries, regardless of currency. It also exists whenever a bank extends credit in any form to borrowers located within the same country but in a currency foreign to that country.

Shared National Credit Program

In 1975, the Office of the Comptroller of the Currency (OCC) instituted a program for the uniform review of shared national credits. A "shared national credit" is defined as any loan in an original amount of $20 million or more that is: (1) shared at its inception by two or more banks under a formal loan agreement; or, (2) sold in part to one or more banks with the purchasing bank assuming its pro-rata share of the credit risk. Beginning in 1977, the OCC was joined in this program by the Federal Reserve System and the Federal Deposit Insurance Corporation. The Federal Reserve carries out the examination of shared national credits of which the lead or agent bank is a state member bank, and the FDIC is primarily responsible for any such credits at state nonmember banks. The OCC supervises review of those shared credits where the lead or agent is a national bank.

National credits should not be analyzed or reviewed at the individual sharing bank. However, on those receiving adverse comment, examiners should review the bank credit files and submit copies of any significant new data that might affect the future classification to Multinational and Regional Bank Supervision.

Although the loan classification, including credits passed, should not be changed, the examiner should consider the effect of material improvement or deterioration in the loss potential inherent in the loan upon:

- The adequacy of the allowance for loan and lease losses.
- The provision for loan and lease losses.
- The overall quality of assets and condition and earnings of the bank.

If the effect is considered significant, the examiner should make appropriate comments in the LPM and/or ALLL narratives.

If examiners are not certain that the credit was reviewed under the uniform program, they should contact their respective field office. Since a minimum number of shared national credits must be originated in any one bank before they are reviewed in the uniform program, examiners in lead banks may find credits eligible for the program, which have not been previously reviewed. If so, examiners should submit a memorandum detailing those credits to the district office to be forwarded to Multinational and Regional Bank Supervision.

Since loans classified as loss under the uniform program must be charged off when such classifications are received by the bank, provisions must be made in the ROE to avoid a double charge-off. The loans will be listed as loss on the "Assets Subject to Criticism" page in the appendix and also on the "Summary of Assets Subject to Criticism" page. An asterisk should be placed by the loss figure and the comment "previously charged off" inserted at the bottom of the "Summary" page. On the statistical data sheet, an asterisk should be placed opposite the figure for losses (item 17). The comment "Does not reflect $ _____ of participated national credits charged off since the last examination" should be inserted at the end of the statistical data sheet.

Interagency Country Exposure Review Committee

In 1979 the Federal Reserve and FDIC joined the OCC in establishing the Interagency Country Exposure Review Committee (ICERC), and the supervisory focus shifted from classifying only banks' specific foreign public sector borrowers to evaluating banks' foreign transfer risk, both public and private. The ICERC categorizes the credits based on the level of transfer risk associated with individual countries reviewed and prepares the write-ups.

ICERC evaluations do not apply to foreign, public, and private loans denominated in the currency of the country where the borrower is located. As a practical matter, ICERC is not in a position to evaluate the financial condition of every borrower, or to determine whether a particular borrower in a country can generate sufficient exchange outside that country to service its own obligations. Therefore, examiner judgment is required to determine commercial credit quality.

Comments for credits classified, credits designated Other Transfer Risk Problems, and credits subject to special comments because of transfer risk are distributed by International Banking and Finance in Washington, D.C. to district management and examiners involved with the international activities of national banks.

Credits that have been classified because of transfer risk problems will be combined with commercial loan classifications used by the three agencies to evaluate a bank's asset quality and financial soundness. Credits that have been placed in the Other Transfer Risk Problems category are not regarded as classified assets. Rather, exposures in this category are considered by examiners as a judgmental factor in their general assessment of a bank's asset quality and the adequacy of its reserves and capital. This is similar to consideration given to such factors as concentrations in the portfolio, the level and composition of Manchurian or reduced rate assets, and management's demonstrated ability to administer and collect problem credits.

Extensions of Credit to "Insiders"

The examiner should make a thorough analysis of extensions of credit to "insiders", i.e., directors, officers, principal shareholders, and their interests. The term "principal shareholder" means any person who owns or controls either directly or indirectly at least 10 percent of the outstanding stock of the designated bank or who owns or controls at least 10 percent of a corporation holding control of the bank. To perform the analysis, the examiner must assimilate information from other areas of examination interest. He or she should consult with examiners responsible for Duties and Responsibilities of Directors, Related Organizations and the other lending areas to determine ownership data and total borrowing relationships. The examiner should note the bank's policy, whether written or implied, relating to extensions of credit to insiders. All "significant" extensions of credit should be reviewed and analyzed for credit quality and compliance with applicable law. For purposes of that review, "significant" is defined as follows:

- If the designated bank has total assets of less than $50 million, any extension of credit which involves an amount exceeding $10,000.

- If the designated bank has total assets equal to or exceeding $50 million and less than $300 million, any extension of credit which exceeds $25,000.

- If the designated bank has total assets equal to or exceeding $300 million and less than $1 billion, any extension of credit which exceeds $50,000.

- If the designated bank has total assets equal to or exceeding $1 billion, any extension of credit that exceeds $100,000.

The examiner should endeavor to determine the existence of any preferential treatment in rate, collateral, repayment terms, or advances beyond paying capacity and any general lessening of normal credit standards. An exact definition of preferential treatment cannot be made. However, any deviation from the bank's normal banking practice for similar credits will dictate further investigation. When preferential treatment is suspected, the examiner should develop all available information supporting that contention.

In the event that a significant transaction with a director, officer, principal shareholder, or a related interest is deficient in any manner (delinquent, criticized, credit or collateral exception, preferential treatment, or violation of law), the examiner should inform senior management of his or her findings and elicit corrective action during the examination. Areas of concern involving insider transactions should be discussed thoroughly during exit review meetings with management and the board of directors. Direct communication with the field manager should precede discussion with the board of directors on serious matters of criticism. All such deficiencies and/or violations of law deserve full comment in the letter to the board of directors. In addition to examination and verification procedures, more detailed guidelines for insider activities are included in the Comptroller's Handbook for Compliance.

Extension of Credit to Brokerage Firms

Many national banks provide lending services to stock brokerage firms using stock of listed corporations as collateral. To promote efficiency in the pledging of collateral, the New York Stock Exchange formed a wholly owned subsidiary, named "Stock Clearing Corporation," to transfer stock ownership through computer book entries and thus eliminate the physical movement of the securities. The operating department of Stock Clearing Corporation, entitled "Central Certificate Service" (CCS), handles the technical aspects of that operation. Brokerage firms deposit shares of eligible securities with CCS. The stock certificates representing those shares are registered in the name of a common nominee. CCS has physical control of the securities while they are on deposit. Loan arrangements are made between the broker and the lending bank with the broker instructing CCS through written authorization to debit the firm's account and credit that of the lending bank. CCS sends a copy of the authorization to the lending bank and will not reverse the entry or make partial withdrawals without written authorization from that institution. Participating banks receive daily printouts showing their position in the program by broker name and type of security. Because of adequately protected controls employed by Stock Clearing Corporation, examiners will accept the daily position printouts without further verification.

Loans to carry investments in commodities entail the same basic criteria as in all credit relationships. Borrowers are typically non-producers or non-processors of the commodity, including individuals, trading companies, manufacturers, or brokers/dealers. The loan may represent a direct investment in the commodity or the carrying of a forward or futures position in the commodity. The commodity being purchased generally secures the borrowing. Common purposes for commodity loans include:

- The temporary holding by a trader of a commodity under contract for sale, or in anticipation of sale in the near term.

- The holding of a commodity by an entity in anticipation of price appreciation for that commodity.

- The holding or inventorying by a manufacturer or fabricator awaiting transformation into some product.

The focus of the examination is on the bank's commodity lending policy and the control exercised over the collateral. The policy should address under what circumstances and conditions commodity loans will be made, particularly whether the bank will grant loans to finance a speculative position in a commodity. For secured loans, collateral margin requirements should be included in the policy.

Control of the collateral is important. Generally, the commodity will be held in a bonded warehouse, bank or other depository. The bank should control title to the commodity. Because commodity markets can become volatile, collateral positions should be monitored frequently for compliance with the policy.

Brokerage firms may borrow to finance their own positions in a commodity, or may be, in turn, financing a client. In the latter case, the dealer reloans the borrowed funds to a customer. In some cases, the loan to the customer may represent credit for margin requirements on forward or futures contracts. Those requirements arise from a price change adverse to the holder's position in the contract. Both speculative and hedged positions require margin funds.

Highly Leveraged Transactions

Banking Circular 242 contains a definition of highly leveraged transactions (HLTs) that has been adopted jointly by the federal bank regulatory agencies. For supervisory purposes, a bank or bank holding company is considered to be involved in a HLT when credit is extended or investment is made in a business where the financing transaction involves the buy out, acquisition, or recapitalization of an existing business. In addition to this purpose test, one of the following criteria must be met for the transaction to be considered an HLT:

- The transaction at least doubles the subject company's liabilities and results in a leverage ratio higher than 50 percent.

- The transaction results in a leverage ratio higher than 75 percent.

- The transaction is designated an HLT by a syndication agent.

In those cases where a credit meets the purpose test but is not covered by any of the secondary criteria, the bank supervisory agencies may nevertheless designate the credit as an HLT.

Most HLTs are repaid by operating cash flow, asset sales, refinancing, sales of stock back to the public, or sale of the company. Cash flow is the most common source of repayment. If operating cash flow is insufficient, other sources of repayment are generally too tenuous to support the loan.

Highly leveraged transactions generally consist of three tiers of financing, including senior debt, mezzanine financing, and equity.

Senior debt has priority over other creditors and equity investors and is the least risky type of HLT financing. However, senior debt exposures in individual transactions are usually much larger than a position in the equity or mezzanine tiers. Thus, the examiner should not take undue comfort because the banking company only participates in senior debt. Reasonable policies, procedures, and controls must be in place, regardless of what portion of the financing package the banking company is participating in. Banks are most often involved as providers of senior debt in the form of term loans, bridge loans, and revolving working capital loans. However, credit risk may also arise through letters of credit and derivative products, such as currency and interest rate swaps. All credit risk should be included in HLT exposure. In a typical highly leveraged transaction one-half to two-thirds of the financing is in the form of senior debt, generally term loans from banks.

Term loans are generally secured by the assets of the target company and its subsidiaries. Bridge loans are short-term loans that provide financing for tender offers while the term financing package is being arranged. Bridge loans extended by banks may or may not be secured, but are generally made on a senior basis. Bridge loans can turn into long-term loans if things do not go as planned. Some banks also provide revolving working capital loans that are secured, often by inventory and/or receivables.

Mezzanine financing refers to portions of the HLT financing package that provide the holder less seniority than senior debt holders, but more standing than equity investors. "Junk bonds" are a part of the mezzanine tier of leveraged financing. Although national banks are able to extend subordinated loans, they are prohibited from holding debt securities that are not investment grade and readily marketable. As a result, national banks have participated less, and generally through their holding company parents or nonbank affiliates, in the mezzanine financing tier. Equity or equity-like financing may be provided by a bank's small business investment company or by the parent bank holding company or a non-bank subsidiary thereof.

Certain risks are common to HLTs, including price risk, management risk, business risk, and interest rate risk. Price risk is the risk of paying too much for the company. Debt service on a HLT is more sensitive to the up-front price than to an equivalent change in interest rates.

Management risk is the risk that management will be unable to manage the company properly. This is important in leveraged financing because the company does not have additional debt capacity to meet unexpected demands.

Business risk is the risk inherent in the economic and business cycle to which every company is exposed.

Interest rate risk is the risk that interest rates will increase and make debt service more difficult than originally envisioned.

More detailed information on HLTs can be found in the Comptroller's April 1989 publication "Leveraged Financing and National Banks." Guidelines to assist examiners in evaluating a bank's HLT activities are contained in Examining Circular 245.

General Procedures

Objective: Determine the scope of the examination for commercial lending.

1. Review the following information to identify if previous problems require follow-up. Determine if management satisfactorily responded to any adverse findings.

   □ Previous ROE.
   □ Supervisory strategy and overall summary comments in the OCC's Electronic Information System.
   □ EIC's scope memorandum.
   □ Bank management's response to previous examination findings.
   □ Previous examination working papers.
   □ Audit reports, and working papers if necessary.
   □ Bank correspondence on commercial lending.

2. From the LPM examiner or EIC, obtain the results of his or her analysis of the UBPR, BERT, and other OCC reports. Identify any concerns, trends, or changes involving commercial lending since the last examination.

3. In addition to the general information requested in the LPM program, obtain and review any other internal reports management uses to supervise commercial lending activities. Examples include:

   □ Loan trial balance, past dues, and nonaccruals for the commercial lending department.
   □ Commercial loans whose terms have been modified by reducing the interest rate or principal payment, by deferring interest or principal, or by other restructuring of the repayment terms.
   □ Commercial loans on which interest is not being collected in accordance with the terms of the loan.
   □ Commercial loans with interest capitalized after the initial underwriting.
   □ Organizational chart of the commercial lending department.
   □ Resumes of commercial lending department management and senior staff.
   □ Copy of the most recent Problem Loan Status Report on each adversely graded commercial loan over a given amount.

4. Obtain from either the LPM examiner or the bank EIC:

☐ Any useful information obtained from the review of the loan and discount (or similar) committee minutes.
☐ Reports related to commercial lending that have been furnished to the loan and discount (or similar) committee, or the board of directors.
☐ Copy of previous examination report pages applicable to commercial lending.
☐ Copies of previously classified and special mention loan write-ups.
☐ List of directors, executive officers, principal shareholders, and their interests.
☐ Any commercial lending line sheets from the previous exam.

When requested information is received, verify its completeness with the request list.

5.   Identify the types of credit present in the portfolio, noting any specialty type lending activity (e.g., SBA loans, HLTs)

6.   Early in the examination process, determine if there have been any material changes in the types of products, underwriting criteria, volume of lending, changes in market focus, etc., through the following:

   • Discussions with executive/senior management.
   • A review of internal bank reports on the commercial lending department.
   • A review of commercial lending policies and/or procedures, paying particular attention to any changes since the previous examination.

7.   Based on the performance of the previous steps, combined with discussions with the EIC and other appropriate supervisors, determine the examination scope. Set Examination Objectives.

Note: Select from among the following examination procedures the necessary steps to meet those objectives. Seldom will it be necessary to perform all of the steps in an examination.

Quantity of Risk

Conclusion: The quantity of risk is (low, moderate, high).

Objective: To assess the types and levels of risk associated with the bank's commercial lending, including an evaluation of the portfolio for quality, collectability, and collateral sufficiency.

1. Obtain the loan trial balance and list of undisbursed loan proceeds.

2. Using an appropriate sampling technique (refer to the "Sampling Methodologies" booklet), pull a sample of loans to be examined in detail. Exclude the bank's basket of small business loans, if one is designated.

3. Check with other examiners in charge of other lending areas to see if they identified any commercial loans in their areas that should be included in your sample.

4. For shared national credits:

    Compare the schedule to the trial balance to ascertain which loans are portions of shared national credits.
    - For each loan so identified, transcribe appropriate information from schedule to line sheets. (No further examination procedures are necessary in this area.)
    - Carry forward risk classification assigned.

5. For loans within the scope of the Interagency Country Exposure Review Committee:

    Compare the schedule to the trial balance.
    - Transcribe country risk rating information from the schedule to the line sheet and return the schedule. No further examination procedures are necessary for public sector credits. However, private sector credits should be reviewed for commercial credit risk.

6. For all sample loans, prepare line sheets which include the following:

    Loan information from requested schedules, noting any loans that are

---

past due or in nonaccrual status.
- Any significant "other asset" balances attributable to each borrower in the sample.
- Liability and other information on common borrowers from examiners assigned cash items, overdrafts, and other loan areas. Determine who will review the borrowing relationship.
- Significant liability and other information on officers, principals, and affiliations of borrowers included in the sample. Where appropriate, cross-reference line sheets to other borrowers.

7. For previously reviewed loan relationships, file the old line sheets with current line sheets.

8. Determine the disposition of any loans classified or criticized at the previous examination. Consider:

    Current balance(s) and payment status, or
    - Date loan was repaid and the payment source.

9. Obtain credit files for all borrowers in the sample and document line sheets with sufficient information to determine quality and/or grade.

10. Assess the credit risk posed by the financial condition of the borrower, on a departmental basis and for individual loans. In your analysis:

    Analyze balance sheet and profit and loss items in current and preceding financial statements, and determine the existence of any favorable or adverse trends.
    - Review components of the balance sheet, as reflected in the current financial statements, and determine the reasonableness of each item as it relates to the total financial structure.
    - Analyze loan commitments and other contingent liabilities.
    - Determine, for seasonal lines of credit, if the trade cycle supports clean-up (complete payout) of that portion of the debt structure.
    - Determine, for permanent working capital loans, if cash flow after debt service, capital expenditures, and other operating needs is sufficient.
      - For secured loans, consider amortization of this portion of the debt consistent with the type of borrower and collateral.

- For unsecured lines of credit, consider the borrower's liquidity sources. Analyze any secondary support provided by guarantors and endorsers.

- Determine, for term loans, if the payment terms are consistent with the type of asset financed and assess whether operating cash flow is sufficient to meet the scheduled amortizing payments.

- Review supporting information for the major balance sheet items and the techniques used in consolidation and determine the primary sources of repayment and evaluate their adequacy.

- Assess the quality of credit file documentation. Examples include:
  - analyses
  - memoranda
  - mercantile reports
  - field audit reports
  - credit checks
  - correspondence

11. Assess credit risk posed by a borrower's collateral, on a departmental basis and for individual loans, by:

Reviewing and testing the accuracy of eligible and ineligible receivables by:
  - Considering delinquencies, affiliate transactions, contra-party accounts, U.S. government, and foreign receivables.

Reviewing and assessing the reasonableness of inventory valuations by:
  - Considering the potential impact of cyclical downturns, new competition, and overproduction that may result in excess, stagnant, or obsolete goods.
  - Determining if liquidation valuations consider differing product types, product cycle, specialty and/or the perishable nature of the inventory.

Reviewing and assessing the valuations of furniture, fixtures, and equipment (FF&E) by:
  - Considering the potential impact of cyclical downturns and new competition that may result in excess, stagnant, or obsolete FF&E.
  - Determining if liquidation valuations consider specialty use of the FF&E.

Reviewing and assessing the valuations of real estate by:
  - Considering the quality of real estate appraisals, evaluations, and other internal valuations. Refer to "Commercial Real Estate and Construction Lending" and/or "Residential Real Estate and Home Equity Lending".

Reviewing and assessing the valuations of other assets (e.g. notes receivable, investments in other businesses) by:
- – Considering management's view on the marketability for the receivable or other asset.
- – Determining if valuations reflect liquidation values.

Analyzing any secondary support provided by guarantors and endorsers.

General Portfolio Review

1. From the results of the loan sample analysis and examination procedures, identify any area with inadequate supervision and/or undue risk, and discuss with bank EIC the need to expand procedures.

2. Test the bank's compliance with established policies for commercial loans. Consider:

   Results of examiner loan file work.
   - Internal exception reports.
   - Internal loan review, audit, and compliance process findings.

3. Determine if any previously charged-off commercial loans have been rebooked. If so, determine that the rebooked loan(s):

   Comply with the bank's policy criteria and terms for granting new loans. Compare interest rates charged to the interest rate schedule and determine that the terms are within established guidelines.
   - Comply with OCC policy on re-booked charge offs.
   - Is not subject to classification.

4. Compare the original amount of the loan with the lending officer's authority.

5. Test the addition of the trial balances and the reconciliation of the trial balances to the general ledger. Include loan commitments and other contingent liabilities.

6. Review accrued interest accounts by:

Evaluating and testing procedures for accounting for accrued interest and for handling adjustments.
- Scanning for any unusual entries.
- Follow up on any unusual items by tracing them to initial and supporting records.

7.   Using a list of nonaccruing loans, check loan accrual records to determine that interest income is not being recorded.

8.   Obtain or prepare a schedule showing the monthly interest income amounts and the commercial loan balance at each month end since the last examination, and:

Calculate yields.
- Investigate significant fluctuations and/or trends.

9.   For participations purchased and sold and loans sold in full since the preceding examination:

Test participation certificates and records, and determine that the parties share in the risks and contractual payments on a pro-rata basis.
- Determine that the books and records properly reflect the bank's liability.
- Investigate any loans sold immediately prior to this examination to determine whether any were sold to avoid possible criticism during this examination.
- Determine if any loan participations are criticized adversely at another participating bank.

10.   For miscellaneous loan debit and credit suspense accounts:

Discuss with management any large or old items.
- Perform additional procedures as deemed appropriate.

11.   Examine notes for completeness, and agree the date, amount, and terms of the note to the trial balance.

12.   Determine that each file contains documentation supporting guarantees and subordination agreements, where appropriate.

13. Determine that any necessary insurance coverage is adequate and that the bank is named as loss payee.

14. Review disbursement ledgers and authorizations to determine if authorizations are signed in accordance with terms of the loan agreement.

Objective: Determine compliance with applicable laws, rulings, and regulations.

1. Test compliance with the following laws, rules, and regulations:

   - 12 USC 84 and 12 CFR 32 – Lending Limits
   - 12 USC 371c – Loans to Affiliates
   - 18 USC 215 – Commission or Gift for Procuring Loan
   - 2 USC 431(8)(B) and 2 USC 441b – Political Contributions and Loans
   - 12 USC 1972 – Tie-in Provisions.
   - 12 USC 1817(j)(9) – Loans Secured by Bank Stock.
   - 12 USC 83 – Loans Secured by Own Stock.
   - 12 USC 582 – Loans Collateralized by U.S. Notes.
   - 12 CFR 221 – Regulation U.
   - 12 CFR 9 – Loans to or Collateralized by Trust Accounts.
   - 12 CFR 211 – International Banking Operations.
   - 31 CFR 103.33(a) – Retention of Credit Files.
   - 17 CFR 17f-1 – Lost and Stolen Securities Program.
   - 12 CFR 400-402 – Export-Import Bank of the United States.
   - 7 CFR 1400-1499 – Commodity Credit Corporation.
   - 12 CFR 200-299 – Agency for International Development.

2. Determine whether any previous examinations of this department have noted any violations of law or regulation. If so, determine whether the bank undertook corrective action.

3. Test subsequent compliance with any consumer law or regulation where violations were found.

Quality of Risk Management

Conclusion: The quality of risk management is (strong, satisfactory, weak).

Policy

Conclusion: The board (has/has not) established effective policies and standards governing commercial lending.

Objective: To determine if the board of directors has adopted commercial lending policies consistent with safe and sound banking practices and appropriate to the size, nature, and scope of the bank's operations.

1. Determine if the board of directors, consistent with its duties and responsibilities, has adopted policies that:

   Define acceptable risks (e.g., product, concentrations) and establish parameters for controlling the risk.
   - Establish procedures for reviewing credit applications.
   - Establish standards for determining credit lines.
   - Define acceptable collateral.
   - Establish standards for determining loan-to-value parameters.
   - Establish minimum requirements for verification of borrower's assets.
   - Establish minimum standards for documentation.
   - Establish minimum standards for monitoring, measuring, and reporting identified risks and associated controls.

2. Determine if management and the board monitor changing market conditions in the bank's lending area to ensure that lending policies continue to be appropriate.

3. Determine if the bank's commercial lending policies are reviewed and approved by the board of directors at least annually.

Processes

Conclusion: Management and the board (have/have not) established effective processes for commercial lending.

Objective: To determine if processes, including internal controls, are adequate.

1. Determine the adequacy of processes designed to identify, measure, monitor,

and control credit risk. Consider the following:

Use of loan agreements and financial/collateral covenants, including monitoring and enforcement.

- Practices for receiving and analyzing timely financial data.
- Systems to ensure that the borrower supplies the required information before funding and periodically thereafter.
- Practices to determine the ongoing accuracy and reliability of borrower certifications that serve as justification for advancing funds.
- Systems for monitoring compliance with loan covenants.
- Methods to enforce and control funds advanced under established LTV advance rates.
- Systems to ensure that collateral first liens are properly perfected and maintained.
- Procedures to monitor ongoing lien status and to continue financing statements.
- Periodic verification of the borrower's accounts receivable and inventory.
- Safeguards to ensure the authenticity of all pledged collateral.
- Adequacy of required collateral inspections and appraisals and whether they are conducted by qualified individuals.
- Control over cash and collateral proceeds.

2.   Determine the adequacy of processes designed to identify, measure, monitor, and control risks posed by the borrower's internal operations.

Does the bank test the accuracy and reliability of a borrower's financial and collateral accounting and reporting systems?

- Does the bank's due diligence process and periodic field audits consider the borrower's ongoing compliance with applicable state and federal laws, rules and regulations? This includes those pertaining to environmental, health, safety and fair labor.

3.   Determine the adequacy of processes designed to identify, measure, monitor, and control transaction risk.

Commercial Loan Records

Considerations:
Is the preparation and posting of subsidiary commercial loan records performed or reviewed by persons who do not also:

- Issue official checks or drafts singly?
- Handle cash?

Are the subsidiary commercial loan records reconciled daily with the appropriate general ledger accounts, and are reconciling items investigated by persons who do not also handle cash?

- Are delinquent account collection requests and past due notices checked to the trial balances that are used in reconciling commercial loan subsidiary records with general ledger accounts, and are they handled only by persons who do not also handle cash?
- Are inquiries about loan balances received and investigated by persons who do not also handle cash?
- Are documents supporting recorded credit adjustments checked or tested subsequently by persons who do not also handle cash? (If so, explain briefly.)
- Is a daily record maintained summarizing note transaction details, i.e., loans made, payments received, and interest collected, to support applicable general ledger account entries?
- Are frequent note and liability ledger trial balances prepared and reconciled with controlling accounts by employees who do not process or record loan transactions?
- Is an overdue account report generated frequently? (If so, how often?)
- Are subsidiary payment records and files pertaining to serviced loans segregated and identifiable?

Loan Interest

Considerations:
Is the preparation and posting of interest records performed or reviewed by persons who do not also:
- Issue official checks or drafts singly?
- Handle cash?

Are any independent interest computations made and compared or tested to initial interest record by persons who do not also:
- Issue official checks or drafts singly?
- Handle cash?

Collateral

Considerations:
Determine whether multicopy, pre-numbered records are maintained

---

that:
- – Detail the complete description of collateral pledged?
- – Are typed or completed in ink?
- – Are signed by the customer?
- – Are designed so that a copy goes to the customer?

Are the functions of receiving and releasing collateral to borrowers and of making entries in the collateral register performed by different employees?

- Is negotiable collateral held under joint custody?
- Are receipts obtained and filed for released collateral?
- Are securities and commodities valued and margin requirements reviewed at least monthly?
- When the support rests on the cash surrender value of insurance policies, is a periodic accounting received from the insurance company and maintained with the policy?
- Is a record maintained of entry to the collateral vault?
- Are stock powers filed separately to bar negotiability and to deter abstraction of both the security and the negotiating instrument?
- Are securities out for transfer, exchange, etc., controlled by pre-numbered temporary vault-out tickets?
- Has the bank instituted a system that:
  - – Insures that security agreements are filed?
  - – Insures that collateral mortgages are properly recorded?
  - – Insures that title searches and property appraisals are performed in connection with collateral mortgages?
  - – Insures that insurance coverage (including loss payee clause) is in effect on property covered by collateral mortgages?

Are coupon tickler cards set up covering all coupon bonds held as collateral?

- Are written instructions obtained and held on file covering the cutting of coupons?
- Are coupon cards under the control of persons other than those assigned to coupon cutting?
- Are pledged deposit accounts properly coded to prevent unauthorized withdrawal of funds?
- Are acknowledgments received for pledged deposits held at other banks?
- Is an officer's approval necessary before collateral can be released or

substituted?

Other

Considerations:
- Are notes safeguarded during banking hours and locked in the vault overnight?
- Are all loan rebates approved by an officer and made only by official check?
- Are all notes recorded on a note register or similar record and assigned consecutive numbers?
- Are collection notices handled by someone not connected with loan processing?
- Are payment notices prepared and mailed by someone other than the loan teller?
- Does the bank prohibit the holding of debtor's checks for payment of loans at maturity?
- In mortgage warehouse financing, does the bank hold the original mortgage note, trust deed or other critical document, releasing only against payment?

Commodity loans or loans to commodity brokers and dealers

Considerations:
Is control for the collateral satisfactory, i.e., stored in the bank's vault, another bank, or a bonded warehouse?
- If collateral is not stored within the bank, are procedures in effect to ascertain the authenticity of the collateral?
- Does the bank have a documented security interest in the proceeds of the future sale or disposition of the commodity as well as the existing collateral position?
- Do credit files document that the financed positions are and remain fully hedged?
- Does the bank maintain a list of the major customer accounts on the brokers or dealers to whom it lends?   If so, is the list updated on a periodic basis?
- Is the bank aware of the broker/dealer's policy on margin requirements and the basis for valuing contracts for margin purposes (i.e., pricing spot vs. future)?

- Does the bank attempt to ascertain whether the positions of the broker/dealer's clients that are indirectly financed by bank loans remain fully hedged?

Personnel

Conclusion: Management and effected personnel (do/do not) display the skills and knowledge necessary to manage the risk inherent in commercial lending.

Objective: To determine whether management and effected personnel display acceptable technical skills in managing and performing duties related to commercial lending.

1. Determine significant current and previous work experience of management and commercial lending personnel. Consider level of experience in specialty areas of commercial lending.

2. Determine whether management and commercial lending personnel are well-educated in commercial lending and whether they plan further education in the subject. Consider:

    Knowledge of potential lender liability issues.
    - Knowledge of the Bankruptcy Code and the specific risks relating to post-petition financing and lien priority.

3. Determine if commercial lending personnel understand and comply with established bank policies, underwriting standards, and documentation requirements. Consider examination results.

Controls

Conclusion: Management has instituted (effective/ineffective) control systems for commercial lending.

Objective: To determine the adequacy of loan review, internal/external audit, management information systems, and any other control systems for commercial lending.

1.   Determine the effectiveness of the loan review system in identifying risk in commercial lending. Consider the following:

   Scope of loan review.
   - Frequency of loan reviews.
   - Qualifications of loan review personnel.
   - Results of examination.

2.   Review the most recent loan review report for commercial lending. Determine if management has appropriately addressed concerns and areas of unwarranted risk.

3.   Determine the adequacy of the audit function for commercial lending. Consider:

   The scope of internal audit.
   - Frequency of reviews.
   Qualifications of internal audit personnel.

4.   Obtain a listing of audit deficiencies noted in the latest review performed by internal and external auditors from the examiner assigned "Internal and External Audits." Determine if management has appropriately addressed noted deficiencies.

5.   Determine if management information systems have the capacity to gather and track information as well as provide needed reports.

Conclusion

Objective: To communicate examination findings and initiate appropriate corrective action.

1. Provide EIC with a brief conclusion memo regarding the quality, level, and direction of risk and the adequacy of risk management systems. Consider:

    The quality of department management.
    *   The quality of loan underwriting practices.
    *   The adequacy of policies and procedures relating to commercial loans.
    *   The manner in which bank officers are operating in conformance with established policy and procedures.
    *   The quality of internal loan grading.
    *   Adverse trends within the commercial lending department.
    *   The accuracy and completeness of the bank's management information system reports for commercial lending.
    *   Internal control deficiencies or exceptions.
    *   The types and levels of risk associated with the bank's commercial lending activities and the quality of controls over those risks.
    *   Commitments received from bank management to address any concerns identified.

2. Determine the impact on the aggregate and direction of risk assessments for any applicable risks identified by performing the above procedures.

Risk Categories:	Compliance, Credit, Foreign Currency Translation, Interest Rate, Liquidity, Price, Reputation, Strategic, Transaction
• Risk Conclusions:	High, Moderate, or Low
• Risk Direction:	Increasing, Stable, or Decreasing

3. Determine in consultation with EIC, if the risks identified are significant enough to merit bringing them to the board's attention in the report of examination. If so, prepare items for inclusion in the Report of Examination under the heading Matters Requiring Board Attention.

MRBA should cover practices that:
- – Deviate from sound fundamental principles and are likely to result in financial deterioration if not addressed
- – Result in substantive noncompliance with laws.

MRBA should discuss:
- – Causative factors contributing to the problem
- – Consequences of inaction
- – Management's commitment for corrective action
- – The time frame and person(s) responsible for corrective action.

4. Prepare a memorandum to the examiner assigned "Loan Portfolio Management" stating your findings. Discuss:

- Quantity of risk
- Quality of risk management
- Delinquent loans, segregating those considered "A" paper.
- Violations of laws, rulings, and regulations.
- Loans not supported by current and complete financial information.
- Loans on which collateral documentation is deficient.
- Concentrations of credit.
- Special mention and classified loans.
- Any concerns and/or recommendations regarding condition of department.
  - – What are the root causes of the problems?
  - – What factors contributed to the less than satisfactory conditions?
- Management's strategies to correct noted deficiencies.

5. Discuss findings with management including conclusions regarding applicable risks. Examiners should discuss all issues listed above, as well as:

- Examination objectives and scope.
- Examination conclusions.

6. As appropriate, prepare a brief commercial lending comment for inclusion in the report of examination. Consider:

- The quantity of risk assumed by the bank from commercial lending exposures. Include an assessment of the impact of the commercial loans' exposure on the nine risk areas.
- The quality of the bank's process to manage risk created in commercial loan exposures.
- The adequacy of policies and procedures.
- The manner in which bank officers operate in conformance with established policies.

7. Prepare a memorandum detailing those loans eligible for the Shared National Credit Program that were not previously reviewed under the program. Include the names and addresses of all participants and the amounts of their credit. (This step applies only to credits where the bank under examination is the lead bank.)

8. Provide either the examiner assigned "Loan Portfolio Management" or the bank EIC with a memorandum specifically stating what the OCC needs to do in the future to effectively supervise commercial lending in this bank. Also include estimates of the time frame, staffing, and workdays required.

9. Prepare a memorandum or update the work program with any information that will facilitate future examinations.

10. Update information in the OCC's electronic information system and any applicable report of examination schedules or tables.

11. Organize and reference working papers in accordance with OCC guidance.